Original title:
Verses from Vine Valley

Copyright © 2025 Creative Arts Management OÜ
All rights reserved.

Author: Amelia Montgomery
ISBN HARDBACK: 978-1-80567-313-2
ISBN PAPERBACK: 978-1-80567-612-6

Chronicles Carried on the Wind

Whispers dance through leafy vines,
A squirrel's chatter, a rooster whines.
Mice scamper, sipping berry juice,
While rabbits argue who's the best moose.

The breeze carries tales of last night's feast,
When grapes played cards, the fun never ceased.
Old tomcat claimed he could outrun a deer,
But tripped on his tail, much to the crowd's cheer.

Reverberations of the Grape Harvest

Frogs serenade from a puddly nook,
While badgers argue 'bout the best grape book.
Chickens laugh, their wings in a whirl,
As the sheep tell tales of a lost pearl.

Bottles clink in the winemaker's hand,
Sipping the sunlight, as they all planned.
The dog rolls in muck, claiming it's wine,
While cats roll their eyes, "Now that's not divine!"

Soft Shadows in the Silken Shade

In a hammock strung between two trees,
A sleepy goat hums a lullaby breeze.
The sun peeks down, a curious spy,
While owls judge from branches up high.

Ducks playing poker with acorns and pine,
Laughing at odds, all sipping moonshine.
The shadows stretch, tickling the ground,
As giggles escape without making a sound.

Kaleidoscope of Kinship and Kiss

Familial squabbles fill up the air,
A parrot's opinion — 'Let down your hair!'
Uncles attempt to juggle ripe fruit,
While a goat yells, "Now that takes some loot!"

Cousins trade secrets behind muck and hay,
While ants march in line, with snacks on display.
The sun sets low, painting skies in glee,
As laughter erupts, unity's decree!

Chronicles of the Autumn Harvest

Pumpkins roll down the lane,
Scaring crows with no shame.
Apple pies float like balloons,
Squirrels plotting raccoon tunes.

Corn mazes twisted and bright,
Lost folks shout with pure delight.
Cider flows like gossip indeed,
Laughter grows like every seed.

Serenade of the Swaying Greens

Greens dance in the breeze so wild,
Radishes play like a playful child.
Lettuce winks from its leafy show,
Even the weeds break out in a glow.

Herbs gossip in whispers and sighs,
Basil and thyme share the latest lies.
A garden party with veggies in tow,
Each plant hoping for a rave glow.

Reflections in the Dew-kissed Morning

Morning dew like jewels at play,
Flowers yawn in a natural way.
Bees buzzing jokes at sun's first gleam,
Nature's laughter flows like a dream.

A squirrel sips coffee from a nut,
While a snail dreams of a speedy cut.
The sun tickles all with its rays,
Here in chaos, the world just plays.

Wanderings Through the Verdant Paths

Down the path where laughter grows,
Each twig's a friend that surely knows.
Frogs croon their tunes, a quirky band,
While butterflies plot a travel plan.

A bush starts dancing, leaves in a twirl,
As a dandelion puffs with a whirl.
Nature's circus puts on a show,
With every step, let your giggles flow.

Murmurs of the Monsoon Harvest

Raindrops dance on thirsty leaves,
A pig in boots, how it weaves!
Squirrels in a raindrop race,
Chuckle in their fluffy face.

Cabbages wear tiny hats,
While chickens chat with chubby bats.
Under fluff of cloud delight,
Everything's funny in twilight.

Dancing beans waltz in style,
Toward cackles, they run a mile.
Fields of corn giggle and sway,
Harvest comes out to play.

Quintessence of the Quickening

See the crops play peek-a-boo,
As they sprout in joyous crew.
Radishes dressed up for a ball,
Inviting every critter, large and small.

Bees charged like tiny cars,
Counting petals, their own stars.
Chipmunks throw disco parties,
While frogs croak rhymes in parties.

Carrots in a tangled hug,
Pulsing like a jovial drug.
Every sprout with a quip so spry,
Under the sun, laughter won't die.

Fables of the Fertile Grounds

In the field, a cow named Lou,
Tells tales of the mud and dew.
Mice plot with adventurous glee,
Having a picnic under a tree.

Tomatoes blushing red with cheer,
Yelling, 'Snack time! We are near!'
Spinach sneezes with a loud pop,
Oh dear veggies, never stop!

Pumpkins throw giant chuckles,
Rolling in their orange buckles.
As gatherers roam with cheer,
The harvest sings—fun is here!

Histories of Hazy Hues

Dandelions debate in the breeze,
Forget-me-nots tease with ease.
Sunflowers strut with floppy smiles,
Walking the fields for miles and miles.

Midnight veggies tell a tale,
Of how they danced in the pale.
Undercover carrots take a bow,
While chill peas whisper, 'Holy cow!'

As night blankets the giggly grounds,
Moonlit laughter — such vibrant sounds.
Wrap up in the joy of dusk,
Filling hearts with sunny musk.

Soft Echoes in the Sunset's Glow.

In the twilight, frogs start to sing,
Chasing fireflies, oh what a fling!
The moon waits, a cheeky old bird,
Whispering secrets, quite absurd.

A raccoon dressed in a fancy suit,
Steals my snacks, oh what a hoot!
His partner, a squirrel in a top hat,
Dances around like a chubby acrobat.

Whispers of the Grape-laden Breeze

The grapes giggle on their vines so high,
Tickled by whispers, they start to fly.
A toad in a tux picks up the phone,
'Hello, party time!'—then he's gone!

Breezes blow tales of wine and cheer,
As bees wear shades, buzzing near.
Bottles pop, corks take a leap,
In a waltz of laughter, secrets they keep.

Secrets of the Twisting Vines

Twisting vines tell tales of great fun,
Of grape-sized mischief under the sun.
Snakes throw parties, they slide and glide,
While rabbits in bowties throw confetti wide.

A hedgehog juggles, a true delight,
With acorns, nuts, and a lightning strike.
Every twist and turn brings fits of glee,
In this vine-clad world, you'll want to be free.

Melodies Among the Leafy Arbors.

Among the leaves, the melodies play,
Singing about the fruity buffet.
A crow in a band, with glasses so bright,
Leads the tune till the fade of night.

Chipmunks twirl in their tiny shoes,
Performing their best, with nothing to lose.
A jam session brews, oh what a sight,
The forest laughs, till the morning light.

Chants of the Clustering Hills

The hills were alive with laughter's cheer,
A goat in a hat sang loud and clear.
Each tree shook its leaves with playful delight,
As squirrels danced round in the soft moonlight.

The grass wore a jacket, a plaid design,
With rabbits debating who'll drink the best wine.
Their jokes flew like kites in the breeze up high,
While clouds chuckled softly as they drifted by.

Nectarine Nights Beneath the Stars

Under the stars, we paint with sweet fun,
A fruit fight erupts, and I'm the chosen one!
With nectarines flying and laughter to spare,
I dodge and I weave, like a kid in mid-air.

The moon, a big peach, winks down from above,
While crickets all chirp to the rhythm of love.
A frog on a lily pad plays a guitar,
And we sing silly songs 'til the sun's on par.

A Palette of Flora and Fauna

In a garden of giggles where flowers chat loud,
A daisy proclaimed, "I'm the prettiest, proud!"
But a dandelion piped in, with a puff of his seeds,
"I'll spread humor far, fulfilling all needs!"

The bees wore small glasses, collecting sweet glee,
While butterflies danced, oh so gracefully!
A ladybug joked, "I'm a dot in a sea,
Of colors and chaos, just like a spree!"

Wind-Whispers Through Wistful Vines

The vines held a conference, so tangled and wise,
Arguing loudly 'bout the juiciest flies.
"I caught one!" said one, with a viney boast,
While the wind rolled in, acting like a ghost.

It whispered sweet secrets, tickling the leaves,
As the grapes all giggled, "Let's play bring and weave!"
Their laughter rang out, a most fruity cheer,
While the breeze added jokes we could all hear!

Harmony in the Harvest

The grapes are dancing on the vine,
With legs like jelly, oh so fine.
A bunch fell down, made quite a scene,
They bounced like balls, so very keen.

The farmer chuckles, reaching wide,
As fruity pranks no longer hide.
The chickens laugh and join the play,
In this grape-tastic, bright array.

The tractor's stuck in a berry jam,
The dog just looks, a worried sham.
But laughter echoes through the field,
A harvest shared, that fate has sealed.

Blessings of the Bramble

Oh, prickly friends, you know so well,
You guard your goodies with a yell.
I came to pluck a berry sweet,
But left with thorns on my bare feet!

The bramble bush just chuckled low,
"Come back again, I'll steal the show!"
I brought my kin, we had a ball,
Until we found we lost it all.

The pie we planned was now a race,
For missing berries left no trace.
We laughed and ran, the chase was on,
With hope that sweetness would return.

Threads of Time in the Vineyard

The old vine whispers tales of yore,
Of grapes that sang and asked for more.
With every grape, a giggle came,
A history rich, a playful game.

The corkscrew twists in pure delight,
As bottles cheer for evening's flight.
Yet, one cork lost its way to roll,
And took a tumble—oh, such a goal!

The glasses clink with silly cheer,
As grapes tell tales we yearn to hear.
With every sip, the laughter grows,
In vineyards where the good time flows.

Odes to the Orchard's Heart

In orchards where the apples grin,
They play hide-and-seek, they win.
A squirrel steals my favorite fruit,
I chase him down in bright red boots!

The blossoms giggle, swaying free,
As bees buzz loudly, "Look at me!"
Each fruit a joke, each branch a jest,
In this sweet orchard, they jest the best.

The pies we bake are filled with love,
Yet envy lingers from above.
The clouds, they hover, grumpy still,
As laughter echoes on the hill.

Whirlwind of the Wine Festival

At the festival, glasses clink,
Dancing grapes in a silly wink.
A cork pops, the crowd lets out cheer,
One fell off the table—oh dear!

Balloons float high, beyond the trees,
A spilled drink brings giggles and wheezes.
The winemakers flaunt their grandest blends,
But lose their hats when the wind bends!

Wobbling folks in a grape-stomp race,
Tripping over their own shoelace.
With every stomp, the juice flies high,
A splash of red, oh me, oh my!

The sun sets slow, the laughter swells,
Tales of grapes, and drunken yells.
In this whirlwind of laughter and fun,
The festival ends—who's next to run?

Expressive Echoes of a Grape's Journey

In the vine's embrace, a grape does grin,
Thinking of someday, where to begin.
From tiny bud to a juicy beast,
Dreaming of parties, to dance and feast.

Rolling through fields with squeaky shoes,
Whispering secrets to the morning dew.
"I'll be a merlot," one grape declares,
While another dreams of fruity affairs!

From barrel to bottle, a journey grand,
With twists and turns, they make their stand.
Grapes gather tales of sun and rain,
And laugh aloud, "Let's do it again!"

In this wild ride, they share their woes,
Of pesky bugs and a farmer's hose.
But laugh they must, these grapes on a spree,
For wine flows better when you're feeling free!

Canvasing the Colors of Wine

Purple hues paint the sky at dusk,
Swirling in glasses, oh what a musk!
Red, white, and rosé dance on the tongue,
As the paintbrush of life, the grapes are flung.

With splashes of color, they come alive,
Each sip a canvas, where flavors thrive.
But watch your step, the ground's a chase,
With splashes of wine, we all lose grace!

A swirl of yellow round the campfire light,
Grapes giggle softly, feeling quite bright.
"We're more than just corked, we want to gleam!
Let's color the world with our juicy dream!"

And as the night fades into the deep,
All the colors promise sweet sleep.
In every glass, a story we find,
A masterpiece waiting, one of a kind!

The Language of the Ripening Fruit

In the garden where laughter grows,
Grapes whisper tales that nobody knows.
"Ripen me quick!" one plump fruit sighs,
As others giggle, "Oh look, it's wise!"

They debate how sweet they'll taste in a glass,
"Let's flirt with sunshine, let's make it a blast!"
Each droplet of dew, a secret shared,
In this wacky vineyard, none are spared.

The sun teases low, the shadows play,
"Let's party tonight!" the ripe grapes sway.
A raucous debate on how red they'll be,
As bees just buzz, "Can't you see?"

In the end, it's all just good fun,
With laughter and juice, life's never done.
So raise a glass to the fruits that delight,
In their own silly language, they shine so bright!

Shadows Beneath the Canopy

In the grove where giggles bloom,
Squirrels dance, avoiding doom.
They drop their nuts—oh what a fall!
Each splash of acorn starts a brawl!

Old grapevines weave a tangled chart,
Telling tales of an aching heart.
A hedgehog won the race today,
But tripped on leaves—what a display!

Sunlight plays on trunks so tall,
A rabbit stole a farmer's call.
The rooster laughed, but he was late,
Forgot to wake 'cause he was fate!

Beneath the boughs, the shadows jive,
Bumblebees sing to keep alive.
Mischief dances in every shade,
In this orchard, joy won't fade.

Tales from the Winding Rows

Rows of grapes, they twist and twine,
A drunken sprout shouts, "Ain't it fine?"
But when the wind begins to sway,
He trips and lands—oh what a play!

A cow named Bessie found a hat,
Declared herself the queen of that!
She sought to wear it, not to munch,
But slipped and flopped—a silly crunch!

The crickets chirp with flair and style,
While frogs compete in the fashion mile.
Each leaf's a cape, each stem a stage,
For critters dressed to win their wage!

In winding paths of nature's fun,
Cabbage critters race till they're done.
In this green realm where laughter glows,
We savor tales of silly rows.

Dreams in the Vintage Soiree

The harvest bash is quite the sight,
A grape gets tipsy, feels just right.
He declared to all, "I am the best!"
Then tumbled down, oh, what a jest!

Chairs made of stalks, a feast on vines,
A dance-off starts with silly signs.
A pumpkin tripped on his own seat,
Now rolls away, that can't be neat!

The cider flows like joyous glee,
But someone spilled it—oh, look and see!
A hedgehog slips, does a little spin,
Laughs with the crowd, and then jumps in!

At midnight's chime, the lanterns sway,
The grapes declare, "Let's dance away!"
In dreams of wine and merriment,
We toast to joy, and what's heaven-sent!

Blossoms Beneath the Harvest Moon

Underneath the moon so bright,
Bumblebees buzz with sheer delight.
They chatter loud, and one slips back,
Plans a dance, but goes off track!

The flowers gossip, share their schemes,
While crickets plan their midnight dreams.
The daisies mock the dandelion,
"Your fluff is great, but scent's the lion!"

A hedgehog wears a floral crown,
Proclaims, "Dear friends, let's win this town!"
But right then trips, the crown does fly,
And all the blooms burst out in sighs!

As harvest moons light up the scene,
Nature's laughs echo, joy unseen.
In this garden of quirky tales,
Life blooms warm in laughter's trails.

Portraits Painted by Nature's Hand

In a garden where the veggies grow,
Tomatoes blush like pros at a show.
Cucumbers sport a jealous green,
While carrots dance, an orange machine.

Sunflowers wave with a goofy grin,
Bees bump around with a buzz and spin.
The radishes giggle, hiding their heads,
While lettuce leaves chatter about their beds.

Pumpkins pose, all plump and round,
With squash nearby, slightly frowned.
A broccoli tree stands tall and proud,
As a pepper struts, wearing a crowd.

At dusk, the critters throw a ball,
While fireflies flash, lighting up the hall.
Nature's art puts smiles in the land,
A party thrown by nature's hand.

Emotions Woven in Tannin's Touch

In a vineyard where the grapes hang low,
The wine knows secrets we'll never know.
Corks pop like jokes that never get old,
While glasses clink, stories unfold.

Chardonnay dreams in a buttery way,
While Merlot laughs at a rolled-up hay.
Pinot grigio flirts with the breeze,
Making blushes in bunches with ease.

Sauvignon blanc sways, fancy and bright,
With a zesty punch, it's out every night.
The tannins whisper, "Let's have a cheer!"
As barrels giggle, "Good times are here!"

In this vineyard, we raise our toast,
To the laughs we've shared, they matter the most.
With each little sip, we find a new clue,
That laughter, like wine, just gets better with you.

Sketches of a Sun-kissed Scene

The sun dangles like a comic show,
With grapes that giggle, row by row.
A bee just tripped, it's quite absurd,
Buzzing tales, not a single word.

Squirrels in shades, lounging with flair,
Debating nuts with a stylish air.
A snail speeds past, all in a rush,
As laughter echoes, there's no need to hush.

Birds chirp a tune, offbeat and sweet,
As they dance around, tapping their feet.
A lazy sun, with a wink so sly,
Seems to chuckle at clouds drifting by.

Here in this nook, joy takes its place,
Every chortle's a giggle's embrace.
Life is a riddle, silly and keen,
In scenes like these, nothing's routine.

Yearning of the Verdant Vale

In verdant fields, the frogs serenade,
Hopping in boots, a funky parade.
The daisies blush at their strange little prance,
While crickets cast votes for the best dance.

A sheep with dreams of becoming a star,
Practices baaa-ing from near and afar.
Each blade of grass sways to the beat,
As squirrels throw cheese puffs for a treat.

Down by the brook, where the fishes tease,
They splash about like they're at a sneeze.
A frog takes a dive, not very sleek,
Flopping around, not a word to speak.

The sky cracks a smile, sun shining bright,
Chasing the shadows, banishing fright.
In this vale, with pleasure abound,
Every second's a giggle, joy knows no ground.

Harmony Amidst the Harvesting

In harvest's thrall, where laughter's rife,
Pumpkins roll like they're in a life strife.
A scarecrow jokes with a crow on his hat,
"Why don't you fly? You're overly fat!"

Tomatoes blush in the patch so grand,
As they gossip quietly, hand-in-hand.
A carrot debates if it's too crunchy,
While radishes chuckle, feeling quite punchy.

Baskets swing low, groaning with cheer,
As veggies conspire to toss out a ear.
One onion cries, it can't take the jest,
"I'll make you weep!" – what a bag of zest.

But all's forgotten as dusk starts to creep,
Around the farm, the laughter does leap.
With nature's bloom in this playful play,
Harvesting giggles, come what may.

Canvas of Craving and Aroma

The chef spins dreams in a pot so wide,
With garlic and butter, they swirl and glide.
A dish takes shape, looking quite bold,
But one tiny sprout refuses to mold.

"Why are you here?" the onions implore,
"Because I'm tiny, and I want to soar!"
They chuckle and roll, what a catchy sight,
As spices jive under the kitchen light.

The tomatoes wobble, declaring a feast,
While the herbs tango, delightful and least.
Peppers join in, all fiery and loud,
Creating a frenzy, gathering a crowd.

In this canvas of flavor, smiles appear,
Whisking up giggles, the mood is quite clear.
In a bubbling pot, life's bright and warm,
Where every bite's a jovial charm.

Syllables of the Silvery Stream

In the stream, the frogs do croon,
Their songs outshine the bright full moon.
A fish jumps up with quite a thud,
Splashing splatters, what a bud!

The turtles laugh, they grin with glee,
Sipping tea as sprightly as can be.
A snail slides by, all slow and grand,
Claiming he's the fastest on land!

Raccoons are plotting a funny heist,
Stealing snacks, oh, they're not polite!
But they slip in mud, oh what a sight,
Rolling around, they take flight with delight.

At twilight, all creatures take their stand,
Joining the chorus, it's all quite planned.
With each silly note, laughter will bloom,
In this merry valley, no room for gloom!

Tales from the Tangle of Twigs

In the tangle where squirrels play,
Nuts go flying, what a wild fray!
Chasing tails, round and round they dance,
Bumping head-on, what a chance!

A wise old owl with glasses so thick,
Tells bad puns, oh, what a trick!
Rabbits chuckle, rolling on the floor,
Laughing so hard, they can't take anymore!

A hedgehog, grumpy, demands some snacks,
But he's lost his way, oh, how it attacks!
With every twist, he bumps a tree,
Blaming the branches, "They're just too free!"

As the sun sets behind the fun,
They share their tales, one by one.
In this tangled mess, joy's never far,
In a nutty world, they're the shining stars!

Chill of the Twilight Bunch

As night creeps in, the crickets sing,
A cool breeze teases, oh what a fling!
Fireflies flicker like stars on the ground,
Dancing bright, no need for a crown.

A raccoon in shades devours a pie,
With crumbs on his face, oh my, oh my!
He winks as he licks his little paws,
Declaring himself the King of the Cause!

The owls hoot jokes, that's their grand game,
While the shadows giggle, oh what a name!
With whispers of wind, the giggles extend,
In the twilight hush, the fun won't end!

Each night's a blast, echoing yays,
In a chill of laughter, it never decays.
Join this bunch, just come and see,
Where giggles spread, wild and free!

Fragrance of Midnight Foliage

In the night, the plants wear perfume,
Tickling noses, wafting in the gloom.
A flower giggles, "What's all the fuss?"
With such zest, they spark a big bus!

Foliage rustles with cheeky pride,
Leaves giggling, swirling side by side.
An owl drapes a towel, quite absurd,
Shouting, "Let's party!" Oh how they stirred!

A mouse with a hat lead the parade,
While all the ferns swayed and played.
With a twist of a vine, they take a stroll,
Growing wild, it's out of control!

As stars gleam bright, laughter will thieve,
Creating tales that none can believe!
In this leafy party, joy fills the air,
With fragrance and fun beyond compare!

Secrets Beneath the Canopy

Under the leaves, a squirrel sneaks,
With acorns tucked in for the week's leaks.
He's got a stash, but here's the twist,
He forgot where it is—what a funny mist!

A hedgehog rolls by, pricking with flair,
Wears yesterday's leaves—does he even care?
He's got style, but critters just stare,
'Is that a fashion or a woodland dare?'

A wise old owl hoots, 'What is all this?'
Sipping on dew hanging from a moss-kissed kiss.
With spectacles perched, he's got it all wrong,
"Who needs drama when you've got this song?"

Each day a new laugh, in the sun they play,
In secret spots where they jump and sway.
The canopy holds tales, cheerful and bright,
Where the critters dance by day and giggle at night.

Melodies of the Movable Feast

Gather round the picnic, there's food galore,
But that sneaky raccoon wants to score.
He lifts the lid, oh, what a thrill,
Only to find a plate of veggie swill!

The ants have organized a conga line,
Marching in step to a tune so fine.
One stumbles, and then it's a pitiful crash,
"Did someone bring the snacks—and not the trash?"

A giggling beetle brings jellybeans bright,
Offers them out as if they'll take flight.
"I swear they're magic!" he says with a grin,
But one too many—now they're stuck in his chin!

The sun starts setting, laughter fills the air,
With food fights breaking out--oh, what a scare!
But as the stars twinkle, the feast shall remain,
A hilarious tale of snacks and good gains.

Dreams in the Dew-soaked Grove

In the grove where moonbeams play hide and seek,
A fox dreams of treats, maybe pizza or leek.
With a giggle he snores, what a funny sight,
Chasing marshmallow clouds in the soft moonlight.

A bear with a cap has cakes on his mind,
Dancing round trees like he's truly unkind.
He trips on a root, what a glorious fall!
Wakes up the trees—'Hey, do you hear my call?'

Eavesdropping owls cackle, "Get a grip, my dear!"
Their raucous laughter echoes far and near.
As the night unfolds with wishes and cheers,
The grove fills with joy, hushed giggles through years.

Dreams dance at dawn, where the humor won't fade,
In the dew-soaked embrace where all antics are made.
With nature in sync and laughter so sweet,
Who knew a nap could feel quite so neat?

Rivulets of Aroma

In the air, sweet whispers of flowers in bloom,
A bee buzzes by, creates quite the room.
He's lost all direction, dizzy as can be,
Thinks he's invented a new dance—what glee!

The herbs in the garden conspire together,
Mint pulling pranks, while sage writes a letter.
"Dear Thyme," says Basil, with humor intact,
"Thank you for all the tips—for that's a fact!"

Tomatoes take turns playing king of the hill,
But rolling away, oh, it's quite the thrill!
"They can't catch us!" they laugh, as they tumble and roll,

What a wild waltz from the garden's own soul!

With rivulets of aroma swirling around,
The garden bursts forth with laughter unbound.
In this fragrant domain, fun thrives and plays,
Where scents become stories in hilarious ways.

The Essence of Earthy Echoes

In a garden where daisies talk,
On every stem, a silly walk.
The carrots wear hats made of cheese,
They giggle and dance in the warm breeze.

A potato with shades, oh what a sight,
Sipping on juice, feeling just right.
The radishes tell jokes, red in the face,
While the lettuce spins, keeping up pace.

The onions are crying, but it's all in fun,
They play tag with the sun, until day is done.
With squashes in capes, they soar in the air,
Every veggie a joker, with laughter to share.

At dusk in the plot, under stars so bright,
The veggies convene for a roast at night.
A feast of laughter, a banquet of cheer,
In this earthy realm, all nonsense is dear.

Pure Whimsy in the Warp of Wind

The clouds wear hats, what a quirky crew,
Dancing in patterns, old and new.
The breeze tells tales of lost kite flights,
While whispers of giggles spark the nights.

A butterfly plays hopscotch, it's true,
Jumping from flower to flower, who knew?
With petals as banners, they float so free,
Cheering the flowers with joyous decree.

The wind is a jester, tickling the trees,
Bending their branches with laughter and ease.
A squirrel on a tightrope, wobbling with glee,
Is this a circus, or just fantasy?

In the swirl of the day, breezy and bright,
Whimsy unfolds like a warm delight.
With a wink and a smile, life turns surreal,
This merry caper makes hearts feel ideal.

Rustling Reveries of Late Afternoon

In the late afternoon, shadows play games,
The sun slips away, but not without claims.
A frog on a leaf, sings out a tune,
While crickets join in, under the moon.

The daisies hold hands, as if in a dance,
Swaying together, lost in a trance.
A spider weaves stories, silk spun with care,
As gossip unfolds in the warm summer air.

The breeze tickles cheeks, with a puff and a laugh,
As birds plot a race—who's fastest? A giraffe?
With laughter erupting from bushes nearby,
The world sprinkles humor like clouds passing by.

As the day waves goodbye, grinning so wide,
All creatures unite for a humorous ride.
In this rustling dream, where chuckles abound,
Joy in late afternoons is happily found.

Songbird Serenade at Day's End

The songbirds gather, what a lively scene,
Singing of mischief, of all that they've seen.
A squirrel requests tunes filled with nuts and delight,
As shadows stretch out, ending the light.

The blue jay cracks jokes, while robins just laugh,
A nightingale's solo, just proof of the gaffe.
Chirping in rhythm, they shake up the night,
Under the glow of the moon, what a sight!

A sparrow wears glasses, looking quite wise,
Debating the truths of the stars in the skies.
With worms as their snacks and giggles galore,
The evening concludes with a raucous encore.

At the end of the day, with hearts feeling fine,
These quirky creatures sip soda and pine.
For tomorrow's adventures of jests to be spun,
In their songbird symphony, joy has begun.

Revelry in the Vineyard's Arms

In a field where grapes do play,
I tripped on vines, oh what a day!
The bottle rolled, the cork took flight,
We laughed until the morning light.

The wine was sweet, the jokes were bold,
With every sip, new tales retold.
The sun beat down, we danced and spun,
In our vineyard dress-up, oh what fun!

A chicken joined our merry throng,
Clucking tunes, it danced along.
With laughter bubbling, we made a fuss,
Who knew the vine could spark such trust?

As dusk rolled in, the moon took heed,
With tipsy hearts, we loved the creed.
To toast to life, with friends and cheer,
In the vineyard's arms, we sold our fear.

The Spirit of Sipping Eras

A clinking cup from days of yore,
We sip the past, then ask for more.
A vintage laugh from time gone by,
Brings echoes of the grape and rye.

With hats too big and shoes askew,
A wise old owl now served the brew.
Each sip a trip through ancient lands,
Where magic swirls in drunken strands.

The grapes debated, red and white,
Which one was best for silly fights?
But in the end, they couldn't settle,
And we all danced like wine-crazed beetles.

To sip is fun, to laugh is grand,
In every glass, a dreamland planned.
So raise your cup, let spirits soar,
In silliness, we find our core.

Elysian Dreams Among the Vines

In twilight's glow, we seek the fun,
Among the rows, we laugh and run.
A grape brigade, in dreams we leap,
With silly songs that make us weep.

The night was filled with quirky sights,
As fireflies danced like disco lights.
We toasted fruits with silly straws,
While sipping wine that sparked applause.

A squirrel joined, thinking it wise,
To sample grapes of every guise.
With tipsy giggles, we shared the cheer,
As he twirled round without a fear.

Elysium here, with friends so dear,
In wine we found the joy sincere.
With every pour, the laughter streams,
In vineyard realms, we chase our dreams.

Cadence of the Wine-soaked Dusk

As day turns into purple haze,
With lush green vines that dance and sway.
We sip our drinks, a merry crew,
Inventing games, old and new.

With every drop, the laughter flows,
We invent grapes with silly clothes.
A jester grape, a queen divine,
Together they dance on the vine.

The dusk arrives, with stars that wink,
We sit and sip, not stop to think.
Every giggle, every cheer,
Adds to the joy that's ever near.

So here's to evenings filled with jest,
In wine-soaked dusk, we're truly blessed.
With every toast, the world's a stage,
In laughter's delight, we turn the page.

Whispers of the Wild Grapevine

In the shade where shadows play,
Grapes gossip about the day.
They chuckle as the sunbeams dance,
While beetles prance in a silly trance.

Bumblebees buzz, making a fuss,
Over ripe grapes, they simply must.
One tripped and fell, what a sight!
Straight into the grape juice, oh what a fright!

Squirrels in hats, oh what a scene,
Holding court on a vine so green.
They toast with acorns to the sky,
Laughing as the breezes sigh.

Underneath this leafy dome,
Nature's laughter feels like home.
With every sip and every quip,
In this wild place, we laugh and slip.

Echoes in the Orchard

In the orchard where the apples fall,
Trees whisper secrets, tiny and tall.
One apple rolled, with a playful grin,
It shouted, "Catch me! Let the games begin!"

Nearby pears wear tiny crowns,
Throwing shade all around the towns.
A couple of plums join in for fun,
They juggle acorns under the sun.

A partridge sings out a silly song,
While the cat in the grass hums along.
With every note, the laughter grows,
As butterflies waltz on their toes.

Fall apples laugh with every breeze,
Shaking off worries, just like leaves.
In this whimsical, fruity retreat,
Every moment here feels so sweet.

Serenade of Sunlit Leaves

Leaves rustling in the sunny glow,
Whispering tales from long ago.
A leaf flipped down, it did a spin,
Caught the breeze, giggled, and grinned.

Twisting vines with flourish and flair,
Spinning yarns like they just don't care.
A sunflower cracked a cheesy joke,
While the daisies burst out, they simply choked.

Breezes tickle each little bud,
As worms waltz in the warm, soft mud.
Silly ants march in a parade,
Beneath the sun, no plans delayed.

With every flutter, every wiggle,
Nature giggles, oh how it tickles!
In this bright and playful scene,
Life dances on, silly and keen.

Twilight in the Vineyard

As evening wraps the vines in gold,
Laughing grapes share tales retold.
A raccoon sneaked in, trying to dine,
Spilled all the juice, oh what a whine!

Fireflies blink like a disco ball,
While shadows creep and the night birds call.
The owl hoots softly, then it winks,
While the grapevines giggle and more mischief thinks.

The sun dips low, casting playful hues,
With grapes discussing afternoon snooze.
A rabbit hops by, with a little dance,
Inviting the stars to join in their romance.

In the cool of night, whispers take flight,
Where laughter hides around each vine's height.
In this twilight world, we all derive,
A silly joy that makes us feel alive.

Dances in the Dappled Shade

Squirrels wiggle in their groove,
Bouncing up and down to prove.
A rhythm tickles leafy boughs,
While poppies shake their leafy vows.

Bees are buzzing like a drum,
Sipping nectar, oh so numb.
They twirl and swirl, a fluffy fest,
While ants parade, they're truly blessed.

Frogs leap high in funky flair,
Splashing water without a care.
With every croak, a laugh they share,
In this wild dance, they're always there.

So join the fun in this bright glade,
Where every critter takes the stage.
With laughter mixed in sunshine's glow,
Together we can steal the show.

Colors of the Canopy

Oh, look at Larry, the lizard green,
In his fancy coat, he's quite the scene.
He struts along the branch with pride,
While bluebirds sing, they gently glide.

Sunflowers stand tall, striking poses,
While daisies chuckle, wearing their roses.
Colors clash like silly friends,
In riotous hues, the fun never ends.

Caterpillars munch on leaves so bright,
Thinking they're kings, what a funny sight!
But when they start to find their wings,
They'll be the stars of all the flings.

Nature painted this playful place,
With quirks and chuckles, it's a race.
Join the palette, splash around,
In this canopy, joy is found!

Refrains of the Rustic Life

Old farmer Joe wears boots with style,
Chasing chickens with a grumpy smile.
Each flap brings giggles all around,
As they scatter, no peace is found.

Cows in the field do silly tricks,
While goats pretend they're gymnastic kicks.
They butt their heads and then they flee,
Creating chaos, oh what glee!

Corn stalks sway, making funny sounds,
Whispering secrets to the ground.
The wind has jokes, it's quite the tease,
Tickling leaves and rustling trees.

So raise a glass of sweet lemonade,
To rustic life and its silly parade.
With laughter echoing through the land,
Here's to the fun, so unplanned!

Notes from the Nature's Songbook

Crickets strum on nightly strings,
While owls hoot of silly things.
A raccoon plays the tambourine,
In shadows, he's the cutest fiend.

Chirping birds with off-key tunes,
Break the silence of bright full moons.
Even flowers sway and hum,
Dancing as if they're the ones to drum.

Clouds join in with puffy bass,
Creating rhythms in a silly chase.
With each soft whistle, a chuckle flows,
Nature's songbook, oh how it glows!

Bring your joy and let it sway,
In harmony, we'll laugh and play.
With every note, let giggles ring,
In this concert, we all take wing.

Whimsy Amongst the Wine

Grapes giggle down the lane,
Their juice a dribble, but no one's plain.
Corks bounce like little frogs,
Making merry with all the logs.

The bottle's neck wears a funny hat,
While glasses hum like a chatty cat.
Each sip spins tales of drunken dreams,
As laughter bubbles in bubbling streams.

Bugs dance a jig with a twinkle bright,
As snails slide in for a slow-motion fight.
With every toast, a curious quirk,
Life's just a joke, written in work.

So raise a glass, let's take a cheer,
To life's odd flavors we relish here.
In this valley, where grapes misbehave,
We find humor, and it's what we crave!

Palettes of Peace in the Patch

In a garden where colors clash,
Tomatoes dance with a flashy splash.
Radishes giggle, hiding in sun,
While carrots worry: 'Are we too fun?'

Honeybees bumble, all in a whirl,
Creating chaos in floral pearl.
Lettuce shouts, 'I'm the coolest green!'
While onions cry, 'Oh, I'm so keen!'

The butterflies wear tutus high,
Flapping wings, oh my, oh my!
Crickets chirp a symphony light,
Under the moon, a comical sight.

It's a patch where peace comes dressed in flair,
Nature's own stand-up—if you dare.
Pick a fruit, laugh with a friend,
In this cheerful garden, the fun won't end!

Aspirations in the Amber Ashes

In the hearth, the embers blink,
Where flames flicker and glasses clink.
Marshmallows dream of toasting flight,
While logs plan a dramatic night.

As smoke swirls up in fancy curls,
S'mores giggle, spreading sweet swirls.
Pinecones whisper tales of the past,
Of fiery days that went by fast.

A raccoon peeks with saucer eyes,
Hoping for snacks and surprise pies.
Every pop and crackle's a show,
Ashes dance; oh, how they glow!

So gather 'round for stories shared,
In the warmth where no one's scared.
Ambition brews in the crackling heat,
In this cozy nook, life's pretty sweet!

Hues of Harmony Through the Breeze

Breezes play with colors bright,
Fluttering wings in pure delight.
Flowers wave, a giggly crew,
They whisper secrets, old but new.

The sun paints tapestries in gold,
While shadows stretch, their tales unfold.
Kites soar high, a dance in the air,
Chasing clouds without a care.

A squirrel flips with acrobatic flair,
Nature's circus, can't help but stare.
With every rustle, laughter spins,
As the world grins—where joy begins.

So let's spin with breeze, join the song,
In this colorful world, we all belong.
From night to day, the fun's alive,
In the hues of harmony, we thrive!

Legends of the Lucid Landscape

In a land where laughter blooms,
Silly shadows leap and zoom.
The grass wears hats made of cheese,
While cows practice yoga with ease.

Rabbits race in flapping shoes,
Squirrels debate the latest news.
A rooster sings in falsetto tone,
As the trees gossip in a hushed drone.

Worms play chess on a bright red leaf,
While bugs hold court, a royal chief.
The sun peeks down, sporting shades,
As clouds giggle in playful cascades.

Each day a new tale unfolds,
With whispers of mischief in the folds.
In this realm where whimsy thrives,
The absurdity truly drives.

Dew-Drenched Musings of Moondust

Beneath a sky of shimmering light,
Stars juggle apples, what a sight!
The moon's a giant lemon drop,
As night critters dance and hop.

Fireflies wink in the twilight haze,
While crickets join in song and praise.
An owl, quite wise, wears a bow tie,
Murmurs secrets to the butterflies.

A silken spider spins a yarn,
About a cat with a penchant to charm.
As grass blades blush with morning dew,
This world spins wildly, unglued and askew.

They laughed and sang till dawn's first light,
In this dreamscape, pure delight.
Where laughter echoes like a sweet refrain,
Absurdity woven in every grain.

Secrets of the Subtle Seasons

Springtime's giggles sprinkle rain,
While flowers make a wild, fun train.
Summer's sun wears a playful grin,
As popsicles melt, inviting a spin.

Autumn struts in with a feathered hat,
Join her parade, all the creatures chat.
Winter snickers, a snowman joke,
As penguins slide, they shimmy and poke.

Each season a fool, a comic delight,
With mischief woven in day and night.
The trees nod along, sharing their spree,
In this playful play, so wild and free.

In laughter's embrace, they find their tune,
Crafting secrets under the watchful moon.
What fun we find in this merry dance,
Each season a jest, a happy chance.

Boughs of Bliss in a Blessed Breach

In a grove where giggles hang,
A chubby squirrel sings and tangs.
Where fruit-flavored breezes flutter by,
And bananas do the cha-cha shy.

Branches sway like dancers around,
While critters gather for a silly sound.
A parrot jokes, a wise old sage,
In this merry, playful stage.

The air is ripe with laughter's cheer,
As apples whisper secrets near.
Underneath the stars' bright beams,
A bizarre spectacle unfolds in dreams.

Life here bounces in blissful glee,
With every branch a comedy spree.
Joy resides in each twist and turn,
In this sacred nook, for laughter we yearn.

Beyond the Blooming Borders

In a garden where the flowers jest,
Bees wear tiny hats, they're dressed for a fest.
Petals giggle and tumble around,
While daisies crack jokes, oh what a sound!

A cat in a sunbeam, planning a scheme,
Dreams of taking over the whole ice cream.
With a whisker-twitch, he's patrolling the land,
Collecting all laughter with a soft, furry hand.

Squirrels debate on who steals the most,
While a turtle plays referee, busy with toast.
The tomatoes sing songs of ripening late,
While cucumbers dance at a viney estate!

Through borders of bloom, laughter sways wide,
Nature's grand circus, with fun as the guide.
Forget all your troubles, come take a look,
At the quirks of this garden, it's quite the good book!

Light Through the Vine-laced Arches

Under arches of vine where shadows do play,
A squirrel slips through, on a very fine day.
He stops for a sip of grape juice with flair,
Winks at a snail who has yet to compare!

The birds up above sing off-key in delight,
While a butterfly flutters, oh what a sight!
A mole pops his head, all dressed up in style,
Claiming it's just for a moment's worthwhile.

A rabbit hops by, with socks that don't match,
Chasing his tail, what a ridiculous catch!
Laughter resounds through the leafy green gates,
As friends gather round, discussing their plates.

As shadows grow long, the sunlight won't fade,
A party of laughter and snacks are well laid.
In arches of vines, life's funny, you see,
Where every day's full of delightful esprit!

Reflections of the Rustic Path

On a rustic path where donkeys trot by,
One wears a backpack—oh my, oh my!
With carrots for snacks and a map made of cheese,
He's searching for treasures under the trees.

Along comes a goat, with stories to share,
Of how she once climbed to the top of despair.
With a laugh and a bleat, she claims to be wise,
But stumbles on rocks, much to all our surprise!

A chicken on stilts offers wisdom to all,
While joking with frogs that come out for a ball.
Together they waltz, in a curious dance,
Making sure every critter has a chance!

The sun sets down low, bringing giggles and cheer,
As friends share their tales for all passers to hear.
In laughter and joy, the path shows its worth,
Where funny reflections of life share their mirth!

Cider Dreams and Grape Evenings

At dusk in the orchard, the apples make plans,
As squirrels exchange gossip, they're big fans!
Cider dreams bubble in kegs made with cheer,
While a raccoon sneaks sips, shushing all near.

Grapes hang like lanterns, all juicy and round,
They gossip about their next crush in town.
With laughter and giggles, they hang from the vine,
Plotting a party that's truly divine!

A hedgehog brings music, a piccolino bold,
As fireflies light up the scene to behold.
With cider cups high, they toast to the night,
In a vineyard fiesta, everything feels right!

As dreams drift like clouds in the twilight glow,
Creatures of whimsy come out for the show.
With cheer in the air and grapes on a beam,
They celebrate living in cider-tasting dreams!

Echoes of the Sunlit Orchard

In the orchard, apples sway,
A squirrel steals, then runs away.
Laughter echoes, birds on high,
They mock the wind and laugh at sky.

Breezes tickle, branches dance,
A bee's sweet joke, in love's romance.
Sunshine glitters, we can tell,
The goofy blooms that wave 'hello!'

Frogs in frogsuits waltz at night,
While fireflies twinkle, pure delight.
A cat in shades, so slick and cool,
Pretends to be a wise old fool.

So raise a glass, let's toast this cheer,
To fruits of laughter, known far and near.
The orchard's charm makes spirits soar,
In silly joy, forevermore.

Lullabies in the Vineyard's Embrace

In the vineyard, grapes take naps,
They dream of juice in bubbly caps.
A rooster sings, but just for fun,
He thinks he's the morning's number one.

Caterpillars on a stroll,
Debate who'll be the fanciest role.
The sun shines bright, with a grin so wide,
As the sleepy vines sway side to side.

Squirrels clink cups of nutty brew,
Under leaves painted morning dew.
Chasing shadows, giggling glee,
Nature's party, wild and free.

So let's toast to every vine,
In this canvas of silly design.
With laughter flowing like fine wine,
Nature's lullabies, all align.

Treasures in the Grape's Lush Hold

In the grape's hold, a secret lies,
Whispers hide beneath the skies.
With rosy cheeks and laughter bright,
Even the leaves join in the light.

The grapevine giggles, sways with glee,
While bees do the cha-cha, can't you see?
A rabbit hops, with treasure maps,
Searching for snacks, in flowery laps.

Crows don hats, they think they're sharp,
Leading the fruit with a little lark.
A pickle parade, oh what a sight,
As veggies dance 'til the moon takes flight.

So gather 'round, let's share a cheer,
For mischief found and silly cheer.
In this lush land where giggles unfold,
There's always treasures to behold.

Ballad of the Ripening Bunches

Bunches ripen, laugh and play,
They wear their wrinkles in a sway.
With lighthearted jokes from the vine,
A fruity circus, oh how divine!

The grapes conspire, a jest they weave,
In the shade, it's hard to believe.
A songbird croons with a cheeky grin,
As the petals blush, their dance begins.

Pigs in bow ties serve cheese so fair,
The mice pull pranks from their hiding lair.
Around the fountain, laughter chimes,
In this wild grape, no need for rhymes.

So raise a cup, let the giggles roll,
In every bunch, there's joy and soul.
With every sip, a story to share,
Of ripening laughs that fill the air.

Elysium in Earthy Expanse

In a field of daisies, how they dance,
A bee in a tux, chasing romance.
With every step, it winks and sways,
Creating a buzz in hilarious ways.

The carrots giggle, dressed in orange bright,
While onions cry, oh what a sight!
In this garden, laughter takes its flight,
As veggies jest under the moonlight.

Spirit of the Sunset Sips

A grapevine whispers secrets untold,
As sunlight spills its liquid gold.
Wine glasses clink, the party's in bloom,
While corks pop off—chaos in the room!

The cheese stands tall, looking quite grand,
As crackers perform in a quirky band.
We toast to spills and laughter galore,
In this silly dusk, we always want more!

Rhapsody of the Ripening

Fruits in a concert, oh what a show,
Bananas on stage, putting on a glow.
A berry sings high, a melon croons low,
The crowd of apples sways to and fro.

The pears gossip, with juicy delight,
As plums throw confetti—a colorful sight!
With every note, the laughter expands,
In this fruity rhapsody, joy understands.

Prism of Petals and Pairs

Two daisies argue, who's the fairest one?
A tulip chimes in, calling it fun.
With petals all fluffed, they wiggle and sway,
As butterflies gasp, 'Oh, what a display!'

A rose rolls its eyes, 'Can't you chill?'
While violets giggle, hearts full to fill.
Among the blossoms, humor runs wild,
In this garden of laughter, we're all just a child.

Revelations of the Fermenting Cask

In casks so round, opinions soar,
A grape's sly grin, can't ignore.
With each small sip, the tales unwind,
Old barrels laugh, it's all hard to bind.

The cork pops loud, a chaotic cheer,
What's that smell? Oh dear, oh dear!
The vintner's dance, a wobbly spin,
Tripping o'er grapes, he laughs with a grin.

Barrels gossip as they roll,
"Who's the best? Let's take a poll!"
A toasty tale of bubbly love,
As laughter bubbles, up above.

In the bright sun, the grapes confer,
Whispering plans to raise a stir.
Who's fermented more, who's gone to waste?
In vine-sauce dreams, all taste is haste.

Starlit Gatherings on Rustic Fences

Under moonlight, the critters plot,
A dance-off of spiders, a fine little knot.
Over the fence, a raccoon sly,
Furiously munching—Oh my, oh my!

The owls hoot with a thoughtful frown,
"Should we point out their mismatched gown?"
The night is young, the giggles shout,
As fireflies flash their little clout.

Cider spills, a sticky delight,
"Trust me," they say, "it's love at first sight!"
Yet ants parade with a tiny boast,
Deciding who's the absolute most.

On a fence carved with tales of old,
The raccoon shares his treasure bold.
A rib-tickling drama, unfold tonight,
In laughter and cheers, the stars stay bright.

Songs of the Forgotten Trellis

Trellis long gone, with tangled vines,
Whisper of grapes, in silly lines.
Beneath the leaves, a squirrel will dance,
Mistaking the grapes for a sweet romance.

He twirls and hops, mischief on toast,
"Watch me climb, I'm the grapevine's host!"
With every thud, the laughter grows,
As the random fruit throws funny bows.

A sip of juice, a giggle divine,
Ripe little buddies, let's toast to the vine!
The laughter bursts from the shade of green,
In songs of silly, nonsense and glean.

The forgotten trellis, a jester in time,
Turns every grape into a chime.
Together they sing flaws and feuds,
Exploding with joy, like happy moods.

Fables of the Ancient Bough

On an ancient bough, a tale takes flight,
Of branches that fought, oh what a sight!
The apple claimed, "I'm juicier, beware!"
While the pear laughed loud, with stories to share.

"Who'll be the fruit to take first place?"
A faux debate, in this leafy space.
With squirrels as judges, they clapped and cheered,
As acorns laughed, all awkward and weird.

"Let's toss it all, and see what sticks!"
They gathered in clusters, pulling their tricks.
Each fruit made a claim, each fruit told a joke,
While birds chirped in, giggling, no smoke.

In fables told 'neath the dusk so grand,
The boughs held court, a merry band.
As dusk settled softly, secrets wouldn't stay,
Trees winked with humor at the end of the day.

Blooming Banter of the Backwoods

In the bramble, a bear ate a pie,
Sassy squirrels danced, oh my, oh my!
Rabbits wore hats, with flair they pranced,
While the wise old owl just chuckled and danced.

A raccoon with dreams of a rock star's fate,
Sings to the moon, never shows up late.
But a fog rolled in with a fresh batch of yeast,
Now the critters are having a moonlit feast!

Chipmunks gossip, with cheeks stuffed and round,
While the blue jays squawk at the fool on the ground.
They all raise a toast with acorns in hand,
To the funny old ways in their quaint little land.

And as dawn breaks, the laughter will linger,
Silly songs spin from a bird's tiny singer.
In this backwood ballet of chatter and cheer,
Every critter knows it's their favorite year!

The Elegance of Emerald Elixirs

In the glade, a frog sips tea with a grin,
Wearing a monocle, he's ready to win.
Crickets in tuxedos, they tap-dance around,
While fireflies twinkle, wearing gowns profound.

A hedgehog declared, with pride in his tone,
"My potion's the finest you'll find in the zone!"
But a skunk made a face when he mixed up the brew,
Now everyone's hiccupping green bubbles, oh boo!

The wise old tortoise hums a sweet song,
While the ants do pirouettes, spinning along.
But a crow flew by, with a feathered flair,
And knocked off the table with an over-the-air!

But laughter erupts as the chaos unfolds,
The froggy continued, even though he's been scolded.
With emerald elixirs causing a stir,
They sip and they giggle, just a charming old blur!

Rustic Rhapsodies in the Moonlight

Under the stars, a pig played guitar,
By the firelight glow, he's a big rock star.
The sheep clap their hooves to the beat of the song,
While the geese honk along, though it feels all wrong.

A goat tried to dance, but tripped on a stone,
With a tumble and roll, he claimed it was 'groan!'
The barn door swung wide, letting laughter flow in,
As night creatures crooned to the moon's cheeky grin.

Then an owl perched wisely and raised a toast,
"To parties like this, who could ever boast?"
The stars winked above, as if cheering too,
While fireflies twirled in their shimmering view.

Rustic rhapsodies filled the air with delight,
An unforgettable night wrapped in pure light.
With joy on the breeze, they all twirled and spun,
In the moon's warm embrace, they danced till they're done!

Harmony of Halcyon Days

In a sunny meadow, the rabbits play chess,
With carrots for stakes in their friendly contest.
While butterflies flutter, amazed at the show,
With giggles and gasps as their strategy grows.

The hedgehog, a referee, wears a bow tie,
Announcing each move with a snicker and sigh.
But a rogue little mouse sneaks in for the win,
And tips over pieces with a cheeky grin!

The sunflowers nod, in approval they sway,
As the bees hum a tune to brighten the day.
With laughter erupting like bubbles in spring,
Every moment together feels just like a fling.

So raise up your glasses, to high-flying dreams,
In harmony shared, each giggle redeems.
For days full of fun are the sweetest of ways,
To cherish the gift of halcyon days!

Ballad of the Borromean Blossoms

In a garden where the silly things grow,
Petunias danced with a pear and a crow.
They giggled and twirled in the soft morning dew,
While daisies debated just who was the cue.

A butterfly slid on a well-oiled vine,
Said, "Have you heard? The radishes whine!"
The roses rolled laughter, all thorns set aside,
As the sun shone brightly on the flowerbed wide.

The tulips held hands, forming a train,
While sunflowers grinned, feeling a bit vain.
Each bloom shared a secret, about the bees' plot,
To steal all the nectar, tie it up in a knot!

At dusk they all gathered, a riotous crew,
With petals ablaze in the warm sunset hue.
They raised tiny glasses filled with fresh dew,
And toasted to chaos, a wild garden view!

Fragments of Forgotten Seasons

The leaves tell tales of a pickle parade,
Where squirrels in hats played charades in the shade.
A wise old oak laughed as the hickories danced,
While the wind spun around, as if it had pranced.

In winter's embrace, the snowmen had charms,
Waving at frosty, old lady alarms.
The ice cubes debated which one was best,
On merry adventures, they put their skills to test.

Spring brought the whirs of the mad ladybug,
Who claimed she once wore a chic winter rug.
With bright, silly hats made for a pond,
They laughed till the sunlight winked and absconded.

In summer's warm grip, the fruit flies held court,
To judge all the berries, their sweet little report.
With each funny moment, the seasons transformed,
In a playful embrace, absurdity warmed!

Resonance of Ripening Fruit

Beneath the loud branches, a tangerine sighed,
"I'm tired of waiting, let's go for a ride!"
The bananas all giggled, swaying like jelly,
As peaches spun tales of a rash little fairy.

The grapevines grew gossip that tickled their skin,
About apples who whispered, they'd love to fit in.
They dreamed of a picnic, where fruit would unite,
And everyone laughed at how wrong they could bite!

With plums as the jester, who wore a bright crown,
The berries proclaimed, "Let's all head to town!"
They rolled in a basket, a fruity parade,
While cherries picked fights, till their stems almost frayed.

As twilight descended, the fruits sang a tune,
Of seeds and sweet harvests beneath the round moon.
With laughter and joy, they danced through the night,
In the orchard of dreams, everything felt right!

Chronicles of the Crimson Bunch

In the vines where the grapes held their raucous debates,
The big berries laughed, playing fanciful mates.
"Let's form a band!" cried the loudest tart fruit,
With grape jelly dreams and a soft berry suit.

They strummed on the tendrils, a funky delight,
While cider took charge, giving tips for the night.
With laughter erupting, the bunch swayed and spun,
Who knew grapes could jam? It was all so much fun!

A rumor spread fast about sparkling cheer,
That a bottle would burst with fizzy good year.
So grapes held on tight, with a comeback so grand,
Wishing for bubbles to burst on demand!

As dawn painted skies in a bright ruby hue,
The grapes shared their stories, each tale tried and true.
With mischief and smiles, the day was reborn,
In the chronicles of joy, the grapes brightly shorn!

www.ingramcontent.com/pod-product-compliance
Lightning Source LLC
Chambersburg PA
CBHW051641160426
43209CB00004B/745